GOR

• • • • •

It Happened In Canada

• • • • •

Scholastic Canada Ltd.

Cover design by: Terence Kanhai

Canadian Cataloguing in Publication Data

Johnston, Gordon, 1920-
It happened in Canada

Originally published as newspaper items.
ISBN 0-590-74069-5

I. Canada - Miscellanea - Juvenile literature.
I. Title.

FC 173.J64 1985   j971'.002   C84-099608-X
F1026.4.J64 1985

MAJESTIC ANIMALS USED FOR ROYAL GIFTS

NEARLY A THOUSAND YEARS AGO VIKINGS OF MEDIEVAL TIMES TRAVELING TO WHAT IS NOW THE CANADIAN ARCTIC, WERE CAPTURING **LIVE** POLAR BEARS.

THE BEARS WERE USED BY NORSE KINGS AS **GIFT PETS** THAT IMPRESSED OTHER EUROPEAN RULERS

A
HUMOROUS LEGEND IS ATTACHED TO A MASK CALLED THE **"GREAT ONE"**

THE MASK WAS USED IN EASTERN INDIAN RITES FOR THE SICK, AND IT REPRESENTED A SPIRIT WHO ONCE CHALLENGED THE CREATOR *HIMSELF* TO A MOUNTAIN MOVING CONTEST. THE CREATOR RESPONDED BY SMACKING A MOUNTAIN UP AGAINST THE GREAT ONE'S NOSE, LEAVING HIM WITH A PERMANENT NOSE TILT AND A SHEEPISH EXPRESSION

A WORLD RECORD 45.9 Kg TROUT

- TAKEN FROM LAKE ATHABASKA, SASK. - 1961

BEESTINGS IS **NOT** THE STINGS OF BEES! *IT'S* THE FIRST MILK GIVEN BY A COW AFTER GIVING BIRTH TO A CALF

DINOSAURS OF MANY KINDS...

...INHABITED WHAT IS NOW ALBERTA & SASKATCHEWAN 100,000,000 YEARS AGO.

WHEN SEAS COVERING THIS AREA RECEDED AND A GENERAL "DRYING UP" PERIOD EVOLVED IT BROUGHT ABOUT THE END OF THESE CREATURES THAT HAD THRIVED IN WHAT WAS A STEAMY JUNGLE ATMOSPHERE.

FOSSILS OF THE LAST DINOSAURS ON EARTH HAVE BEEN FOUND IN THE AREA AROUND **DRUMHELLER, ALTA.**

A FLYING BATHTUB

When Regina was struck by the giant tornado in 1912 — one man was taking a bath and the bathtub was flung from his disintegrated house and sent flying for half of a kilometer to land on the roof of the Wascana Hotel

THE DOMESDAY BOOK

An authentic copy of this famous book (compiled in 1087) is in Fredericton, N.B.

Johnston—

BLASPHEMY WAS A CRIME IN PIONEER FRENCH CANADA.

AS EARLY AS 1636 A CANADIEN WAS PUNISHED IN A PILLORY FOR THIS OFFENCE

SCALLOPS USE A FORM OF JET PROPULSION TO TRAVEL FROM PLACE TO PLACE — BY OPENING AND CLOSING THEIR SHELLS

"TIMBER"

ONE OF CANADA'S FIRST IMPORTANT COMMERCIAL INDUSTRIES WAS LUMBERING. FAR UP THE MIGHTY RIVERS, HUGE RAFTS OF SQUARED LOGS WERE ASSEMBLED BY THE LOGGERS IN PREPARATION FOR THE SPRING JOURNEYS DOWNSTREAM. WITH THEIR LIVING QUARTERS ON THE DECK, MANY MEN WORKED, SLEPT and ATE ON THE WAY DOWN TO PORTS WHERE THE RAFTS OF SQUARED TIMBER WERE DISASSEMBLED and LOADED ON SHIPS BOUND FOR ENGLAND. *AS EARLY AS 1790, A TIMBER RAFT FROM NEAR KINGSTON, ONT. REACHED QUEBEC CITY*

LOG TROUGH ROOFS

FROM THE EARLIEST DAYS OF FRENCH SETTLEMENT IN THE EAST TO RELATIVELY RECENT TIMES IN THE WEST, ROOFS OF HOLLOWED HALF LOGS WERE USED. THE BARK WAS LEFT ON AND IT IS SURPRISING HOW LONG THEY LASTED WITHOUT CRACKING OR BECOMING NON-WATER SHEDDING

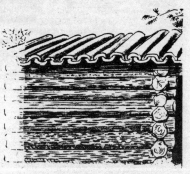

THE ACTION IN
THIS DRAWING
IS INACCURATE

LIKE MANY OTHER INDIAN CUSTOMS, THE USE OF THE
BASIC BOW AND ARROW IS INACCURATELY PORTRAYED
BY WHITE PERSONS · FROM THE EARLIEST SKETCHES ON
DOWN THROUGH MANY YEARS OF HOLLYWOOD EXTRAVA-
GANZAS INDIANS HAVE BEEN DEPICTED SHOOTING THEIR BOWS
IN THE CLASSIC STANCE OF THE EUROPEAN ARCHERS OF THE
MIDDLE AGES. *FOR MANY YEARS LEADING INDIANS LIKE
CHIEF DAN GEORGE OF BRITISH COLUMBIA HAVE CON-
SISTENTLY POINTED OUT THAT INDIANS HELD THEIR
BOWS HORIZONTALLY — NOT VERTICALLY LIKE ROBIN HOOD*

COILED BASKETS
MADE BY INTERIOR SALISH
INDIANS (B.C.), WERE SO TIGHTLY
WOVEN THEY WERE USED
AS COOKING VESSELS

OO-OOH!... THAT'S BETTER

MYRIADS OF ITCHY BUFFALOES FOUND WELCOME RELIEF AT THIS NATURAL RUBBING POST SITUATED IN THE VALLEY OF THE MILK RIVER IN SOUTHERN ALBERTA. THE RUBBINGS OF COUNTLESS BISON CAUSED THE STONE TO ASSUME A 'MUSHROOM' SHAPE

IF WE DID NOT AS BROTHERS LIVE, LET US HERE AS BROTHERS LIE

INSCRIPTION OVER THE ENTRANCE TO THE OLD GRAVEYARD FOR INDIANS AND EUROPEANS —LA RONGE, SASKATCHEWAN

FORESIGHTED **CLÉO SOUCY**

Chief Parliamentary STONE CARVER

AMONG THE **TEN** CARVED SHIELDS OVER THE ORNATE ENTRANCE THROUGH THE PEACE TOWER TO THE CENTER BLOCK OF THE PARLIAMENT BUILDINGS THERE WAS, FOR MANY YEARS, A **BLANK** ONE.

THE OTHER NINE SHIELDS BORE THE COATS-OF-ARMS OF THE PROVINCES OF CANADA. SOUCY HAD PERSUADED THE ARCHITECTS TO INCLUDE THE 10TH BLANK. *THEN AFTER HOLDING OUT FOR 82 YEARS NEWFOUNDLAND ENTERED CONFEDERATION IN 1949 AND M. SOUCY HAPPILY FILLED IN THE BLANK*

BECAUSE OF **CONSERVATION** THERE ARE *MORE BEAVERS* **NOW** THAN WHEN EUROPEANS FIRST ARRIVED HERE

THE FIRST PERMANENT WHITE SETTLEMENT in AMERICA, North of MEXICO, WAS PORT ROYAL —

— BUILT in 1605 by DE MONTS, from PLANS by CHAMPLAIN.

THEFT of A GERANIUM PLANT WAS PUNISHABLE IN EARLY UPPER CANADA BY 5 YEARS IN PRISON

THE **First EARTHQUAKE** ON RECORD IN CANADA OCCURRED IN **1638**. WHAT BECAME KNOWN AS THE **"GREAT EARTHQUAKE"** HAPPENED IN **1663**. CONTEMPORARY RECORDS TELL OF "DOORS OPENING AND SHUTTING BY THEMSELVES WITH A FEARFUL CLATTER; THE BELLS RANG WITHOUT BEING TOUCHED; BUILDINGS SPLIT ASUNDER; FLOORS SEPARATED AND FELL DOWN; CRACKS IN FIELDS HAD DEEP PRECIPICES, AND MOUNTAINS SEEMED TO MOVE OUT OF THEIR PLACES. MANY SMALL RIVERS DRIED UP, IN OTHERS, THE WATER BECAME SULPHUROUS AND OTHERS CHANGED COURSES. TREES WERE UPROOTED AND THROWN CONSIDERABLE DISTANCES. MIDWAY BETWEEN **Tadousac** AND **Quebec** TWO MOUNTAINS FELL DOWN AND THE **Island aux Coudres** ROSE UP AND ALMOST DOUBLED IN SIZE"

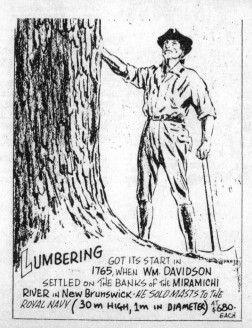

LUMBERING GOT ITS START IN 1765, WHEN **Wm. DAVIDSON** SETTLED ON THE BANKS OF THE **MIRAMICHI** RIVER IN **New Brunswick**. *HE SOLD MASTS TO THE ROYAL NAVY* (30 m HIGH, 1 m IN DIAMETER) AT $680. EACH

BON APPETITE
1855

ON CHRISTMAS DAY, 1855 THE SIMPSON FAMILY OF TORONTO — GRANDPARENTS, A BACHELOR SON, 2 DAUGHTERS WITH HUSBANDS AND 7 CHILDREN WADED THROUGH FOUR TIMES THE AMOUNT OF FOOD THAT A LIKE SIZE FAMILY WOULD CONSUME TODAY.

THIS IS WHAT THEY ATE

BREAKFAST:- LAMB CHOPS, TOAST, PORK PIES, DEVILLED KIDNEYS, HUGE BOWLS OF PORRIDGE AND COFFEE.

DINNER:- 4 KINDS OF SOUP: OYSTER, CHICKEN, GUMBO AND MUTTON BROTH. BOILED BEEF, PORK, MUTTON, TURKEY, POTATOES. CARROTS, TURNIPS, PARSLEY AND ONIONS. **MAIN COURSE:-** 11 ROASTS: BEEF, PORK, MUTTON, TURKEY, VENISON, 3 CHICKENS AND 3 GEESE. **DESSERT:-** TRIFLES, SUET PUDDING, A HUGE PLUM PUDDING, 4 KINDS OF FRUIT CAKE AND 3 KINDS OF WINE. LOZENGES, SUGARED ALMONDS, FRUIT DROPS, BARLEY SUGAR RINGS.

SUPPER:- HAM, VEAL, PORK, BEEF, CHICKEN, TURKEY, HEADCHEESE, 7 KINDS OF FRUIT JELLY, CHEESE, WINE AND A DOZEN PIES AND CAKES

WILD *Turkeys...*

... COULD BE BOUGHT IN 1800 *for* 6¢

The First CIRCUS

TO TOUR AREAS OF CANADA THAT WERE POPULATED WAS RICKETT'S OF LONDON, ENGLAND (COMPLETE WITH WILD ANIMALS AND CLOWNS). IT GAVE ITS PREMIERE PERFORMANCE AT Quebec IN 1798

DOUGHSTON.

SOD HOUSES

WERE OFTEN THE FIRST HOMES OF MANY EARLY PRAIRIE SETTLERS. A TYPICAL SOD HOME USED 45 TONNES OF SOD IN ITS CONSTRUCTION

A BLACK FLAG WAS RAISED ON THE DOME OF MONTREAL'S SOMBER BORDEAUX JAIL EACH TIME AN EXECUTION TOOK PLACE

A TENACIOUS TUNA

THE LONGEST CONTEST ON ANY RECORDS, BETWEEN MEN AND A TUNA FISH, OCCURRED NEAR LIVERPOOL, NOVA SCOTIA, IN 1934.

6 MEN TAKING TURNS, FOUGHT THE 358 Kg TUNA IN A TERRIFIC BATTLE THAT LASTED 62 HOURS

"RIDING A MAN UPON A RAIL"

WAS JUSTICE HANDED OUT BY MID-19TH CENTURY COUNTRY PEOPLE. IT FELL ON THOSE WHO INFRINGED REGIONAL OR MORAL LAWS. *THE CULPRIT WAS STRIPPED OF CLOTHING AND COVERED WITH PINE TAR, ROLLED IN FEATHERS, THEN PLACED ASTRIDE A FENCE RAIL.* THUS, TARRED AND FEATHERED IT WAS UNDERSTOOD HE WOULD NOW LEAVE TOWN

1970 — JONNSTOO

A Vow THAT WAS KEPT

MAISONNEUVE, FOUNDER of Montreal in 1642 WORRIED WHEN THE ST. LAWRENCE RIVER FLOODED THE FOLLOWING SPRING, and HUGE CAKES OF ICE THREATENED THE SETTLEMENT WITH DESTRUCTION. HE VOWED THAT IF GOD WOULD CAUSE THE WATERS TO RECEDE HE WOULD CARRY A CROSS TO THE TOP OF MOUNT ROYAL.

WHEN THE FLOOD ABATED MAISONNEUVE FULFILLED HIS VOW. HE STRUGGLED UNDER THE WEIGHT OF A HEAVY WOODEN CROSS TO THE HIGHEST POINT OF THE MOUNTAIN WHERE HE ERECTED IT — AND DOWN TO THIS DAY A CROSS HAS STOOD THERE

LE CANADA —
BUILT IN 1738

THE FIRST IMPORTANT SHIP TO BE BUILT IN CANADA — THOUGH SHIPS HAD BEEN BUILT IN VARYING SIZES SINCE 1606 — SHE SAW SERVICE WITH THE FRENCH NAVY

©1971 — COLLERSTONE

ITINERANT SHOEMAKERS

— TRAVELED FROM HOUSE TO HOUSE BEFORE SETTLEMENTS WERE DEVELOPED IN UPPER CANADA (ONTARIO).

CARRYING THE TOOLS OF THEIR TRADE THEY BOARDED WITH A FAMILY UNTIL ALL ITS SHOES WERE REPAIRED OR NEW ONES MADE, AND THEN MOVED ON TO THE NEXT HOUSE FOR A REPEAT PERFORMANCE

NORTHERN FLORAL ABUNDANCE

Herschel Island, OFF THE Yukon COAST, THOUGH ONLY A SILT DEPOSIT ON A FOUNDATION of GLACIAL AGE ICE, HAS **370 VARIETIES of WILD FLOWERS**

THE SWAN HAS MORE FEATHERS THAN ANY OTHER TYPE OF BIRD.

ONE WAS FOUND BY ACTUAL COUNT TO HAVE OVER **25,000 FEATHERS**

©1970- JOHNSTON

A **DEER** CAN LEAP A 2·4 m HIGH FENCE *FROM A STANDING START*

THE **NORTH POLE** HAS JUST **ONE** SUNRISE — *MARCH 21* AND **ONE** SUNSET — *SEPTEMBER 21* EACH YEAR

THE MANLY ART OF SELF DEFENCE

FIST FIGHTS OCCURRED BETWEEN INDIVIDUALS IN ALL AREAS OF EARLY CANADA. SCORES WERE SETTLED BY MILITARY PERSONNEL, VOYAGEURS, LUMBERJACKS, MINERS ETC. OCCASIONALLY A FORMAL MATCH WAS ARRANGED AND THE PARTICIPANTS WERE VERITABLE GLADIATORS. THEY FOUGHT W/THOUT GLOVES IN ROUNDS OF 3 MINUTES (SOME MATCHES LASTED FOR 72 ROUNDS) AND ONLY A KNOCKOUT ENDED A CONTEST. THE MARQUIS OF QUEENSBURY RULES WERE INTRODUCED IN 1867—WITH A LIMIT OF 15 ROUNDS

THE GROUNDHOG, WHEN IT IS EXCITED, TAKES 100 BREATHS A MINUTE — YET WHEN HIBERNATING IT BREATHES ONLY ONCE IN 5 MINUTES.

The First NOVEL WRITTEN IN CANADA

WAS THE "HISTORY OF EMILY MONTAGUE", BY **FRANCES BROOKE**.

SHE WAS THE WIFE OF THE CHAPLAIN OF THE GARRISON AT QUEBEC BETWEEN 1763 & 1768, AND THE BOOK GIVES GRAPHIC SKETCHES OF LIFE IN QUEBEC DURING THAT PERIOD

JOHNSTON

BREAKFAST

FOR A PIONEER RURAL FAMILY IN UPPER CANADA INCLUDED: PORK, HONEY, CHICKEN, SALTED SALMON, GINGERBREAD, PICKLED CABBAGE, POUND CAKE AND GREEN TEA

JUST 50 YEARS AGO— MORE THAN **3,000,000** HORSES WERE BEING USED ON CANADIAN FARMS

A LIFE THAT WAS SAVED

JOHN MOLSON

AN EIGHTEEN-YEAR-OLD ENGLISH IMMIGRANT WAS *RESCUED* FROM A MID-ATLANTIC SHIPWRECK AND EVENTUALLY REACHED MONTREAL IN **1782**. HERE HE BUILT AN INDUSTRIAL EMPIRE INCLUDING THE THEN LARGEST BREWERY AND DISTILLERY, CANADA'S FIRST STEAMBOAT AND FIRST RAILWAY

A **TURTLE** CAN LIVE A YEAR *WITHOUT* FOOD

THE **SAMPSON**

WAS THE FIRST STEAM LOCOMOTIVE IN THE MARITIMES — 1839.
IT RAN FROM STELLARTON TO PICTOU HARBOR, NOVA SCOTIA

HEADSTONE
HOOCH
HIDEAWAYS

FOR SOME TIME AFTER 1845 VENTURESOME MEMBERS OF THE CHURCH OF ST. JOHN IN THE WILDERNESS AT NEW GERMANY, NOVA SCOTIA, STORED MOONSHINE LIQUOR IN HOLLOW METAL GRAVE MARKERS IN THE CHURCHYARD.

MEETING THEIR CUSTOMERS AFTER SERVICES THEY SLID BACK THE NAME PLATES AND PRODUCED THE ILLICIT REFRESHMENT FROM THE INNER SPACES OF THE MARKERS

A BOY HERO

WHILE STRONG MEN HESITATED JOE CRACKER of HERRING COVE, N.S. PLUNGED INTO HEAVY SEAS TO RESCUE SURVIVORS FROM H·M·S· "LA TRIBUNE" THAT FOUNDERED AND WAS WRECKED OFF TRIBUNE HEAD, N.S. in 1797. JOE CRACKER WAS JUST 13-YEARS OLD!

A TIME WHEN IT WAS HARD TO TELL THE LEFT FOOT FROM THE RIGHT

PRIOR TO 1820 BOOTS (AND SHOES) WERE FASHIONED THE SAME FOR EITHER FOOT · THERE WERE NO "LEFTS" OR "RIGHTS". GRADUALLY AN IDEA of KING GEORGE IV's, THAT BOOTS SHOULD BE SHAPED FOR EACH FOOT, WAS UNIVERSALLY ACCEPTED

A SALMON STOPPER

ONLY SOMETHING FORMIDABLE CAN PREVENT SALMON FROM TRAVELING UP RIVERS TO SPAWN · HELL'S GATE CANYON AT THE MOUTH OF THE FRASER in B.C. DID. SO MANY SALMON WERE POUNDED TO DEATH TRYING TO OVERCOME THIS OBSTACLE THAT CONSERVATIONISTS FINALLY BUILT FISHWAYS TO CARRY THE SALMON AROUND THE RAPIDS TO THEIR SPAWNING GROUNDS

THE SETTLERS THAT DISAPPEARED

FRUITFUL IN UNITY

Kelowna IS THE ONLY CITY IN BRITISH COLUMBIA THAT HAS A COAT-OF-ARMS THAT IS AUTHENTIC: i.e ISSUED BY THE COLLEGE OF HERALDS AND SIGNED BY THE KINGS-AT-ARMS.

THE LEFT SUPPORTER, A BEAR, REPRESENTS THE ORIGIN OF THE NAME KELOWNA, THE ABORIGINES NAME FOR GRIZZLY BEAR

MORE AND MORE EVIDENCE IS BEING GATHERED TO SHOW THAT *NORSEMEN APPEARED* OVER OUR EASTERN HORIZON IN THE YEARS IMMEDIATELY PRECEDING E. FOLLOWING THE YEAR **1000.** THERE IS ALSO A BELIEF THAT OVER A HUNDRED YEARS BEFORE THEM – i.e. **875** – *CELT-IRISH* MONKS CAME HERE VIA ICELAND AND LANDED ON Brion Island IN THE GULF OF ST. LAWRENCE.

SETTLING IN A PLACE CALLED **Huitramannaland** (COUNTRY OF THE WHITE MEN) BY SCANDANAVIAN WRITERS, ON CAPE BRETON ISLAND, THEY WERE COMPLETELY CUT OFF FROM THE REST OF THE KNOWN WORLD AND WERE GRADUALLY ABSORBED BY THE NATIVE MICMAC POPULATION

©1971 JOHNSTON

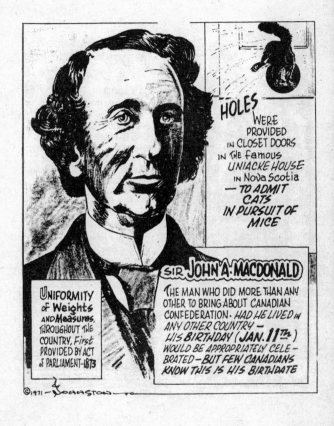

HOLES WERE PROVIDED IN CLOSET DOORS IN THE famous UNIACKE HOUSE IN Nova Scotia — TO ADMIT CATS IN PURSUIT OF MICE

UNIFORMITY of Weights AND Measures, THROUGHOUT THE COUNTRY, First PROVIDED BY ACT OF PARLIAMENT—1873

SIR JOHN A MACDONALD
THE MAN WHO DID MORE THAN ANY OTHER TO BRING ABOUT CANADIAN CONFEDERATION. HAD HE LIVED IN ANY OTHER COUNTRY — HIS BIRTHDAY (JAN. 11TH) WOULD BE APPROPRIATELY CELE-BRATED — BUT FEW CANADIANS KNOW THIS IS HIS BIRTHDATE

©1971 — JOHNSTON —

THE DRIVER OF A "DEADCART"

IN 1832 DAILY WENT FROM HOUSE TO HOUSE IN MONTREAL CALLING OUT "HAVE YOU ANYONE TO SEND TO THE BURIAL GROUND?"

CHOLERA HAD STRUCK A SAVAGE BLOW THAT YEAR AND MANY HUNDREDS DIED. IN MONTREAL THE DEAD WERE HASTILY BURIED IN AN 18TH CENTURY CEMETERY, THEN ON THE EDGE OF THE TOWN.

TODAY THAT CEMETERY LIES BENEATH THE HUSTLE AND BUSTLE OF MODERN DAY TRAFFIC IN MONTREAL'S FAMED DOMINION SQUARE

A **LABORER** IN CANADA IN 1644 RECEIVED AS HIS WAGES, APPROXIMATELY 30¢ A DAY, WITH BOARD

LIGHT for THE WORLD

KEROSENE AND THE KEROSENE OR COAL-OIL LAMP ARE DEFINITE CANADIAN INVENTIONS.

IN 1846 DR. ABRAHAM GESNER AT CORNWALLIS, NOVA SCOTIA, DEVELOPED A PROCESS FOR DISTILLING "KEROSENE" AS HE CALLED IT, FROM A COAL-LIKE MINERAL, ALBERTITE. LATER IT WAS TO BE POPULARLY CALLED COAL-OIL.

UP TO 1846, THE BEST LIGHTING FUEL WAS SPERM WHALE OIL AND THE BEST LAMP WAS A WHALE OIL LAMP. THEN KEROSENE LAMPS BECAME THE LAST WORD IN LIGHTING AND WERE WIDELY USED, PARTICULARLY IN CANADA.

IN 1854, GESNER PATENTED HIS PROCESS AND FORMED THE NORTH AMERICAN KEROSENE GAS LIGHT Co. AND *THE WHOLE WORLD MOVED INTO A KEROSENE AGE*

NEST EGG

ART TIPPET - Windsor, Ont.

WHILE LOOKING FOR BIRD'S NESTS TO MAKE COLOR SLIDES *FOUND A $5 BILL IN ONE*

THE SORCERER

JEAN PIERRE LAVALLEE

IN 1711, LAVALLEE, LIVING ON THE ISLAND OF ORLEANS (NEAR QUEBEC CITY) WAS CREDITED WITH WRECKING 8 BRITISH WARSHIPS BY SORCERERY.

WHEN SIR HOVEDEN WALKER SAILED UP THE ST. LAWRENCE WITH A HUGE FLEET HE RECKONED WITHOUT LAVALLEE, A KNOWN SORCERER, WHO WENT TO WORK WITH HIS SPELLS AND INCANTATIONS. HE PRODUCED A FOG SO THICK IT CAUSED THE BRITISH SHIPS TO DRIFT ON TO ROCKS ... THE SURVIVING SHIPS WITHDREW

THE TOWN THAT MOVED

IN THE 1940'S THE TOWN OF LYNN LAKE *WASN'T*; IT WAS THE TOWN OF SHERRIDON, 264 KM TO THE SOUTH IN THE FROZEN MUSKEG LAND OF NORTHERN MANITOBA. SHERRIDON WAS A MINING TOWN, BUT THE ORE RAN OUT. LYNN LAKE HAD NICKEL ORE — MILLIONS OF TONS OF IT — BUT NO ONE TO GET IT OUT.

SO THEY *JACKED UP* SHERRIDON, PUT IT ON SLEDS AND *WINTER-HAULED IT* BY TRACTOR, THE 264 KM TO LYNN LAKE

WHAT IN THE WORLD ARE YOU DOING FOR HEAVEN'S SAKE?

A **SIGN** IN FRONT OF A PRESBYTERIAN CHURCH — MONTREAL

"UNDER THE SPREADING CHESTNUT TREE"

PIONEER PEOPLE OF EARLY CANADA USED TO GET TOOTHACHES TOO. WITH NO DENTISTS AVAILABLE THEY CALLED ON THE LOCAL BLACKSMITH WHO HAD THE KIND OF TOOLS NEEDED TO PULL OUT THE OFFENDING MOLARS

THE McINTOSH APPLE TREE

In 1796, John McIntosh planted an apple orchard in Dundas County, Upper Canada (Ontario). The seeds weren't reliable and the resulting growth made this plain. Only one tree showed promise. But careful crossing and grafting from the single good tree brought the other trees along.

Today, every McIntosh apple grown can be traced back to the seeds and grafts of the lone tree that John McIntosh nurtured to bring forth the world famous apple named after him

After **Louis Riel** was hanged in **Regina** in **1885** an enterprising (?) merchant sold "souvenirs" of "the rope that hung Riel". The demand was so great he had to obtain nearly a tonne of hemp rope from Winnipeg

THE PHANTOM of PERCE ROCK

FOR MANY YEARS PEOPLE BELIEVED (POSSIBLY SOME STILL DO) THE FAMED PERCE ROCK IN THE GULF OF ST. LAWRENCE WAS HAUNTED BY A YOUNG BRIDE-TO-BE. ON HER WAY TO MARRY A FRENCH OFFICER AT QUEBEC HER SHIP WAS CAPTURED BY PIRATES, AND WHEN SHE REBUFFED ADVANCES MADE BY THEIR LEADER SHE WAS ABANDONED ON THE ROCK AND MANY PEOPLE CLAIMED THEY SAW HER EACH NIGHT AT SUNSET. LEGEND MAINTAINS THE PIRATE SHIP TURNED TO STONE AND BECAME PART OF THE ROCK

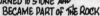

LYNX SKINS

WERE *LEGAL TENDER* AT VARIOUS TIMES *DURING* THE FRENCH RÉGIME

- OUR GREATEST WOMAN ARTIST -

EMILY CARR
1871 - 1945

BORN IN VICTORIA, B.C., SHE STUDIED PAINTING IN CALIFORNIA and EUROPE — THEN WORKED FOR YEARS WITHOUT RECOGNITION IN CANADA. DISCOURAGED SHE QUIT PAINTING FOR 15 YEARS, BUT TOOK UP HER BRUSHES AGAIN AFTER MEETING MEMBERS OF THE NOW FAMOUS GROUP of SEVEN. *TODAY HER PAINTINGS ARE REPRESENTED IN ALL MAJOR CANADIAN COLLECTIONS*

THE **HARVESTER ANT** CAN EASILY PUSH ASIDE STONES THAT OUTWEIGH IT **50** TIMES OVER

GOLD IN NOVA SCOTIA

STORIES ABOUT THE PRODUCTION OF GOLD IN NOVA SCOTIA (FIRST DISCOVERED THE SAME YEAR, *1849*, AS THE FAMOUS CALIFORNIA GOLD RUSH) ARE OVERSHADOWED BY BIGGER STRIKES IN OTHER PROVINCES AND TERRITORIES.

A MAN NAMED **JOHN CAMPBELL** WAS THE FIRST TO PAN GOLD ALONG THE SHORES OF HALIFAX COUNTY. HE AND THE HUNDREDS OF GOLD SEEKERS WHO FOLLOWED HIM NEVER MADE FORTUNES

YET NOVA SCOTIA'S PRODUCTION PER MAN AND GOLD YIELD PER TON WAS BETTER THAN THAT OF EITHER CALIFORNIA OR AUSTRALIA

THE WHITE MAN BROUGHT DEATH

IN 1781 **NINE** OF EVERY **TEN** MEMBERS OF THE CHIPEWYANS, AT ONE TIME THE LARGEST ATHAPASKAN-SPEAKING TRIBE OF THE CENTRAL SUBARCTIC, *DIED OF SMALLPOX* — *A WHITE MAN'S DISEASE*

THE CRICKET
— NATURE'S THERMOMETER

IF YOU SUBTRACT **40** FROM THE NUMBER OF CRICKET CHIRPS A MINUTE AND DIVIDE THE RESULT BY **4** AND ADD **50** TO THE RESULT— *YOU CAN TELL THE TEMPERATURE*

WHEN THE "PEN" WAS MIGHTIER THAN THE SWORD

PRE-CONFEDERATION SCHOOL CHILDREN MADE INK FROM THE SAP OF MAPLE TREES, COPPER SULPHATE, AND IN WINTER TIME, A LITTLE WHISKEY TO PREVENT THE MIXTURE FREEZING. *TO OBTAIN PENCILS THEY POUNDED OUT AND SHARPENED TO A POINT — LEAD BULLETS*

CANADA'S FIRST MAJOR RAILWAY DISASTER

CARRYING ABOUT ONE HUNDRED PASSENGERS, A GREAT WESTERN RAILWAY TRAIN WAS TRAVELING FROM TORONTO TO HAMILTON ON MARCH 12, 1857.

NEARING THE BRIDGE OVER THE DESJARDIN CANAL (UNITING THE TOWNS OF DUNDAS & BURLINGTON, ONT.), THE ENGINE JUMPED THE SWITCH AND FOLLOWED BY THE WHOLE TRAIN TUMBLED INTO THE ICY WATER BELOW.

59 PERSONS LOST THEIR LIVES

THE PHEASANT
CAN LIVE FOR A MONTH WITHOUT EATING

Covered Bridges
(SOMETIMES CALLED KISSING BRIDGES)

DOTTED THE COUNTRYSIDE THROUGHOUT UPPER AND LOWER CANADA AND THE MARITIMES IN PIONEER DAYS (300 STILL REMAIN IN QUEBEC) THEY WERE COVERED TO PRESERVE THE TIMBERS, WHICH IF LEFT OPEN WOULD LAST ONLY ABOUT TEN YEARS, AND NOT TO KEEP SNOW OFF THE DECK. AS A MATTER OF FACT, SNOW HAD TO BE CARRIED IN AND SPREAD AROUND TO ALLOW SLEIGHS TO PASS THROUGH

MUD IN THE EYE OF OFFICIALDOM

IN 1858, ONE JOHN BUTT ARRIVED IN VICTORIA, B.C. AND TOOK UP THE JOB OF CLEANING STREETS UNDER SEPARATE CONTRACTS. SOME TIME LATER OFFICIALS DISCOVERED THEY WERE BEING CONNED. BUTT'S MODUS OPERANDI CONSISTED OF LOADING HIS CART ON GOVERNMENT ST., THEN DRIVING AROUND THE CORNER TO YATES ST. WHERE HE SLYLY LET THE MUD AND FILTH OOZE OUT. RETURNING WITH MORE LOADS HE DISPOSED OF THEM THE SAME WAY.

AFTER CLEARING UP GOVERNMENT ST. HE WOULD OBTAIN A CONTRACT FOR THE MUD HE HAD DEPOSITED ON YATES ST., THEN CART IT BACK TO GOVERNMENT ST. — AND SO ON...

CANADA'S MOST AMAZING ESCAPE-ARTIST

HENRY MORE SMITH

A CONFIDENCE MAN WHO OBTAINED A LIVING BY PRACTICING DECEPTION & THIEVERY IN THE MARITIMES, MAINLY NEW BRUNSWICK, AT THE TURN OF THE 19th CENTURY. NO JAIL COULD HOLD HIM, NOR COULD CHAINS, LEG IRONS AND HANDCUFFS. ONCE JAILED IN KINGSTON, N.B. FOR HORSE STEALING (THE PENALTY FOR WHICH WAS DEATH) HE ESCAPED FROM A MADE TO MEASURE IRON COLLAR THAT WAS FASTENED TO A HEAVY TIMBER FLOOR BY A THICK CHAIN AND A LONG STAPLE. NO ONE EVER LEARNED HOW HE MANAGED TO DO IT

HERE LIES
EZEKIAL
AIKLE
- AGE 102
THE GOOD
DIE YOUNG

GRAVE STONE —

EAST DALHOUSIE CEMETERY, NOVA SCOTIA

CANADA'S FIRST GAMES of GOLF

AFTER THE ARDUOUS SIEGE OF QUEBEC (1759), HIGHLAND OFFICERS OF WOLFE'S ARMY RELAXED BY PLAYING GAMES OF GOLF, A SPORT DEVELOPED MANY YEARS PREVIOUSLY IN THEIR SCOTTISH HOMELAND. THESE WERE THE FIRST GAMES OF GOLF TO BE PLAYED IN CANADA

MAPLE SAP

FLOWS FREELY FROM AN OPENING IN A MAPLE TREE LEFT BY A BRANCH TORN OFF BY FIERCE MARCH WINDS. A SQUIRREL WITH A SWEET TOOTH WILL SEE THAT THE FLUID ISN'T WASTED

LE BEAU DANSEUR

THE HANDSOME DANCER

THE LEGEND OF THE HANDSOME DANCER, ONE OF THE MOST PERSISTENT IN CANADIAN FOLKLORE, WAS PASSED FROM GENERATION TO GENERATION OF EARLY QUEBECERS.

IT FIRST APPEARED IN PRINT IN **1837** AND TELLS THE STORY, WITH VARIATIONS FROM TIME TO TIME, OF HOW THE **DEVIL**, DRESSED IN THE HEIGHT OF FASHION APPEARS AT VILLAGE DANCES TO DANCE WITH THE PRETTIEST GIRLS.

AS LATE AS **1952** THIS HARDY PERENNIAL WAS GOING THE ROUNDS AGAIN, THIS TIME AT ROUTHIERVILLE, QUE. AND CAMPBELLTON, N.B. SO WIDESPREAD WAS GOSSIP OF *THE MANIFESTATION, CANADIAN PRESS FILED A STORY DULY RE-PORTING THE LATEST NEWS OF THE HANDSOME DANCER*

GODERICH, ONTARIO – FOUNDED BY THE CANADA COMPANY IN THE **1820s** HAD INTERESTING TOWN PLANNING. IT WAS LAID OUT IN A STAR FORMATION WITH ALL STREETS RADIATING FROM A CENTRAL SQUARE—

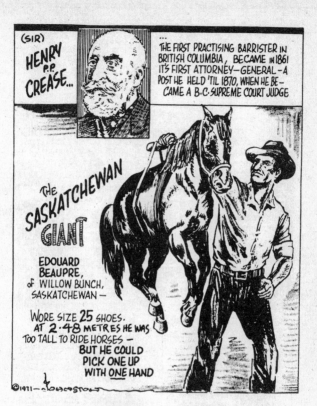

(SIR)
HENRY
P.P.
CREASE...

...THE FIRST PRACTISING BARRISTER IN BRITISH COLUMBIA, BECAME IN 1861 IT'S FIRST ATTORNEY—GENERAL—A POST HE HELD 'TIL 1870, WHEN HE BE-CAME A B.C. SUPREME COURT JUDGE

The SASKATCHEWAN GIANT

EDOUARD BEAUPRE, of WILLOW BUNCH, SASKATCHEWAN —

WORE SIZE 25 SHOES. AT 2.48 METRES HE WAS TOO TALL TO RIDE HORSES — BUT HE COULD PICK ONE UP WITH ONE HAND

©1971—

4-7

CANADA IS THE ONLY COUNTRY IN THE WORLD THAT HAS HAD A CONTINUOUS SERIES of BIRTH RECORDS FOR MORE THAN THREE CENTURIES-- DATING FROM THE CODE of LAWS ISSUED IN QUEBEC IN 1621

HALLOWEEN 'HIGH' JINKS

A STANDARD **GOLD BRICK** CAN BE POUNDED INTO A THIN SHEET LARGE ENOUGH TO COVER ·4 HECTARES OF GROUND

WHEN CANADA WAS STILL LARGELY AN AGRARIAN NATION, YOUTHFUL EXUBERANCE SURFACED ON ALL HALLOW'S EVE NO LESS THAN THAT EXPRESSED BY MODERN YOUTH.

A FAVORITE PRANK OF THOSE BY-GONE DAYS WAS TO PLACE A NEIGHBORING FARMER'S WAGON ON TOP OF HIS BARN

THE SOLDIER WHO WAS A WOMAN

SARAH EDMONDSON

RAISED IN YORK COUNTY, NEW BRUNSWICK, SARAH ENLISTED IN A REGIMENT OF THE UNION ARMY USING THE ALIAS FRANKLIN THOMPSON, DURING THE AMERICAN CIVIL WAR. SHE SERVED FOR TWO YEARS AND CLOSELY ESCAPED DEATH MANY TIMES. SHE WAS THE FIRST WOMAN TO RECEIVE A PENSION FROM THE U.S. ARMY AND WHEN SHE DIED SHE WAS BURIED IN A MILITARY CEMETERY WITH FULL MILITARY HONORS

A VOTIVE LAMP GIVING *PERPETUAL* LIGHT

...LIT IN 1717 BY NUNS IN THE CONVENT OF THE URSULINES, QUEBEC, *IT IS, 257 YEARS LATER, STILL BURNING BRIGHTLY*

THE GIRL WHO FLEW ON THE WINGS of THE WIND

NEAR Milton, Ont. YOUNG *ELIZA HARRISON* WAS HANGING OUT A WASHING ONE DAY IN 1823. SUDDENLY A TORNADO TORE THROUGH THE AREA AND THE STORM BROKE WITH INDESCRIBABLE FURY, FILLING THE AIR WITH FLYING DEBRIS AND DUST. WITNESSES, PEERING OUT OF SHELTERED PLACES SAW *ELIZA* AND THE CLOTHES LINE WHIRLING IN THE AIR ABOVE THE TREE TOPS — YET THE FEROCIOUS WINDS SET HER DOWN NEARLY A KILOMETRE AWAY WITHOUT SO MUCH AS A SCRATCH

THE **LONGEST**
UNDERSEA CABLE
IN THE WORLD
RUNS FROM
PORT ALBERNI, B.C.
TO
**AUCKLAND,
NEW ZEALAND.**

AMERY GIROD...

...COMMITTED
SUICIDE IN **1837.**
UNTIL HIS DEATH
SUICIDES WERE
DENIED A CHRISTIAN
BURIAL, AND THEIR
ULTIMATE FATE WAS
INTERMENT AT A
BUSY CROSSROADS.
*GIROD WAS
THE LAST RECORDED
SUICIDE TO MEET
THIS FATE, AND HE
WAS BURIED AT THE
NOW VERY BUSY
CORNER of GUY
and SHERBROOKE
STREETS in
Montreal*

©1970 — JOHNSTON

FUEL FOR THE CAMPFIRES OF EARLY TRAVELERS ACROSS THE CANADIAN PRAIRIES WAS **BUFFALO MANURE.** *BUFFALO CHIPS OR COW'S WOOD, AS SOME CALLED IT, WAS OFTEN THE ONLY FUEL AVAILABLE ON THE TREELESS PLAINS*

THE *FIRST* MOTOR VEHICLE LICENSE PLATES IN CANADA (ISSUED BY ONTARIO) IN 1903 *WERE MADE OF PATENT LEATHER*

MAUREEN GODSON

OF EDMONTON,

STARTED LEARNING HOW TO FLY IN 1953, WHEN SHE WAS 9 YEARS OLD.

BY THE TIME SHE WAS 10 SHE WAS A PROFICIENT FLYER

— CANADA'S YOUNGEST PILOT

QUEEN VICTORIA STRANGE AS IT MAY SEEM IN THESE DAYS OF INSTANT COMMUNICATIONS, IT WAS MORE THAN A MONTH AFTER THE DEATH OF WILLIAM IV IN 1837 BEFORE CANADA LEARNED ITS SOVEREIGN WAS NO LONGER WILLIAM, BUT VICTORIA

THE MAN WHO HAD A PREMONITION OF HIS OWN DEATH

RECORDED ONLY BY THE NAME OF CARPENTER, HE WAS WITH A PARTY OF "OVERLANDERS" ON THEIR WAY TO THE B.C. GOLD FIELDS IN 1862 WHEN THEY REACHED TURBULENT RAPIDS IN THE FRASER RIVER. HE HUNG HIS COAT ON A TREE BEFORE HEADING INTO THE RAPIDS WHERE HE WAS LOST IN THE SWIRLING WATER. LATER A NOTE WAS FOUND IN HIS COAT POCKET. IT READ: "ARRIVED THIS DAY AT THE CANYON AT 10 a.m. AND DROWNED RUNNING THE CANOE DOWN. GOD KEEP MY POOR WIFE"

MOUSTACHES

WERE WORN BY ALMOST ALL OF THE EARLY MEMBERS OF THE NORTH WEST MOUNTED POLICE (R.C.M.P.). THE REASON, AS GIVEN BY AN INSPECTOR OF THE TIME, WAS THAT THE MEN BELIEVED SHAVING THE UPPER LIP WEAKENED THE EYES

©1973 — Townsend

A HORRIBLE HOBBLER

WAS USED IN JAILS AND PENITENTIARIES IN THE 19ᵀᴴ CENTURY.

KNOWN AS THE OREGON BOOT IT WEIGHED 4·5 Kg AROUND ITS TOP WAS A CIRCULAR 6·8 kg WEIGHT THAT LOCKED AROUND A CONVICT'S LEG

IT'S NOT THAT LONG AGO THAT POLICEMEN IN CANADA'S LARGE CITIES WORE UNIFORMS THE SAME AS THOSE OF BRITISH BOBBIES

TOTEM POLES

ARE FOUND ON THE NORTH PACIFIC COAST, AMONG THE TSIMSHIAN, THE HAIDA AND THE KWAKIUTL TRIBES. THERE ARE TWO TYPES: *MEMORIAL POLES*, USED PARTICULARLY BY THE TSIMSHIAN, COMMEMORATED DEAD MEMBERS OF THE FAMILY, AND WERE SET APART FROM HOUSES. *HOUSE POLES* WERE HERALDIC SIGNS, SYMBOLIZING FAMILY ANCESTORY AND TRIBAL TRADITIONS. THESE WERE ERECTED IN FRONT OF HOUSES. THE ENTRANCE TO WHICH WAS SOMETIMES, LIKE THIS HAIDA POLE, THROUGH A HOLE AT THE BOTTOM

A COOL BRUIN

WHEN IT GETS HOT IN THE MOUNTAIN VALLEYS AND FLIES & SUN BECOME UNBEARABLE — *BEARS THAT LIVE IN MOUNTAIN REGIONS HEAD TO HEIGHTS WHERE SNOWDRIFTS GIVE COOL COMFORT*

THE COFFIN THAT CAME HOME

CHARLES COGHLAN, BORN IN PRINCE EDWARD ISLAND IN 1841 BECAME A DISTINGUISHED ACTOR IN THE U.S.A. HE ONCE VISITED A FORTUNE TELLER WHO TOLD HIM HE WOULD DIE FAR FROM HOME IN AN AMERICA CITY, BUT HE WOULDN'T REST UNTIL HE RETURNED TO THE PLACE OF HIS BIRTH. IN 1898 HE DIED SUDDENLY IN GALVESTON, TEXAS, AND WAS BURIED THERE. TWO YEARS LATER A VIOLENT HURRICANE STRUCK GALVESTON AND THE CEMETERY WAS WASHED INTO THE GULF OF MEXICO.

EIGHT YEARS LATER P.E.I. FISHERMEN FOUND COGHLAN'S COFFIN — IDENTIFIED BY A SILVER PLAQUE — FLOATING OFFSHORE. HE HAD COME HOME AT LAST, 4800 Km FROM WHERE HE DIED AND WAS FINALLY LAID TO REST IN THE PLACE OF HIS BIRTH

THE CANADIAN CHESS ASSOCIATION WAS FORMED IN 1872 IN Hamilton, Ontario

THE TABOO TWO

EARLY AMERICAN IMMIGRANTS TO THE CANADIAN PRAIRIES HAD A STRONG DISLIKE FOR TWO-DOLLAR BILLS. THIS AVERSION HAD ITS ORIGIN IN A 19TH CENTURY U.S. ELECTION IN WHICH CANDIDATES FOR OFFICE BOUGHT VOTES FOR $2 EACH. AS A CONSEQUENCE, ANYONE WITH A $2 BILL WAS UNDER SUSPICION OF HAVING SOLD HIS VOTE. *EVEN TODAY TWO DOLLAR BILLS ARE RARELY SEEN IN THE PRAIRIE PROVINCES, YET ARE WIDELY CIRCULATED ELSEWHERE*

A YOUNG ENGLISH IMMIGRANT NAMED **WILLIAM PRATT** JOINED A TOURING STAGE COMPANY IN **1910** AT *KAMLOOPS, BRITISH COLUMBIA.* HE INVENTED THE NAME **BORIS KARLOFF** FOR HIMSELF AND WENT ON TO BECOME FAMOUS AS THE **FRANKENSTEIN MONSTER**

TUGBOAT ANNIE

— BETTER KNOWN TO MOVIE FANS AS **MARIE DRESSLER**, WAS BORN **LEILA KOERBER**, AT Cobourg, Ont.-in 1860. SHE WON AN ACADEMY AWARD AND AVERAGED A NEW PICTURE EVERY TWO MONTHS FOR FOUR YEARS — YET HER MOVIE CAREER DIDN'T START UNTIL SHE WAS OVER **70** YEARS of AGE

THE FATHERS of CONFEDERATION

REALLY WANTED TO CALL THE NATION THEY FOUNDED **"THE KINGDOM of CANADA"**.

BUT BECAUSE THE USA, NEARLY 100 YEARS AFTER THEIR WAR AGAINST KING GEORGE III WAS STILL SENSITIVE TO THE WORD KINGDOM, THE FATHERS SUBSTITUTED THE WORD **DOMINION**

AFTER THE CELEBRATED PAINTING BY ROBERT HARRIS

GASOLINE WAS, AT ONE TIME, *THROWN AWAY*

BEFORE THE DEVELOPMENT OF THE INTERNAL COMBUSTION ENGINE AND THE MOTOR CAR THERE WAS NO USE FOR GASOLINE. YOU COULD HAVE ALL THE GAS YOU WANTED IF YOU WOULD HAUL IT AWAY FROM THE REFINERIES

A **CHARACTER** CALLED **HOLY JOE**

USED TO WANDER IN MID-WINTER THROUGH THE STREETS OF EARLY *Prince Rupert, B.C.* — *IN HIS BARE FEET*

FAMINE

STRUCK QUEBEC — JUST PRIOR TO THE CONQUEST. PEOPLE VAINLY WATCHED FOR RELIEF SHIPS FROM APRIL 1757 TO MAY 1758 WHEN AID FROM FRANCE MANAGED TO ELUDE THE BRITISH BLOCKADE.

THE POPULACE HAD BEEN REDUCED TO A DAILY RATION OF TWO OUNCES OF BREAD, AND THOUGH THEY ATE THEIR HORSES HUNDREDS DIED OF STARVATION

AN EYE FOR AN EYE AND AN _EAR FOR DEBT_

IN THE ROUGH AND TUMBLE PERIOD BETWEEN THE AMERICAN REVOLUTION AND THE WAR of 1812 ... IT WAS A CUSTOM TO CUT OFF AN EAR OF A PERSON WHO FAILED TO HONOR A DEBT TO ANOTHER

POISSON D'AVRIL (APRIL FISH) IS THE TERM USED BY FRENCH SPEAKING CANADIANS FOR *APRIL FOOL*

A-24

THE **JINX SHIP**
THAT BROUGHT
THE CABLE
TO *HEART'S CONTENT*
NEWFOUNDLAND

THE **GREAT EASTERN**

THE GIANT SHIP THAT LAID THE
FIRST ATLANTIC CABLE FROM EUROPE TO N. AMERICA (ARRIVING AT
HEART'S CONTENT, NEWFOUNDLAND IN 1866) WAS A JINXED SHIP.
IT TOOK 3 MONTHS TO LAUNCH HER, AFTER WHICH SHE UNDERWENT
EXPLOSIONS & MUTINIES THAT KILLED 3 DOZEN MEN. MANY PEOPLE
CLAIMED SHE WAS CURSED BECAUSE 2 RIVETERS HAD BEEN SEAL-
ED INTO HER HULL DURING HER CONSTRUCTION. OTHERS RIDICULED
THE IDEA THAT THIS COULD HAVE HAPPENED... *BUT WHEN THE HUGE
LEVIATHAN WAS BROKEN UP FOR SCRAP, IN 1889, WORKMEN*
DISCOVERED TWO SKELETONS* WITH *RIVETER'S TOOLS.

A DANGEROUS OCCUPATION

WAS THAT OF FIREMEN ON THE EARLY TRAINS. THEY HAD TO FREQUENTLY CRAWL ALONG THE RUNNING BOARD AS THE ENGINE THUNDERED ON ITS WAY, TO PLACE GREASE IN ALL THE BEARINGS. *THE WORK WAS ESPECIALLY DANGEROUS IN FREEZING OR OTHER KINDS OF INCLEMENT WEATHER*

GOAT ISLAND

WHICH SEPARATES THE CANADIAN AND AMERICAN FALLS AT NIAGARA DERIVED ITS NAME FROM THE FACT THAT ITS *FIRST* OWNER **JOHN STEDMAN,** *USED IT TO PASTURE A GOAT*

THE LUCK OF THE DRAW

WHEN THE UNITED EMPIRE LOYALISTS ARRIVED IN UPPER CANADA (ONTARIO) THEY WERE GIVEN LAND BY A FAIR AND DEMOCRATIC PROCESS. *THEY DREW THEIR LOT NUMBERS FROM A HAT HELD BY A CROWN ADMINISTRATOR*

DANIEL HARMON

IN 1811 STARTED THE FIRST FARM WEST OF THE ROCKY MOUNTAINS, NEAR FORT ST. JAMES. *GOOD YIELDS OF POTATOES, TURNIPS AND BARLEY WERE OBTAINED*

THE MOST
COLOSSAL
UNDERSTATEMENT
IN
HISTORY

Francois Marie
VOLTAIRE
1694-1778

—FAMED FRENCH WRITER
AND PHILOSOPHER, WHO
ON LEARNING THAT CANADA
HAD BEEN TAKEN FROM
FRANCE BY BRITAIN, SAID
IT WAS NO GREAT LOSS·
AFTER ALL, CANADA
WAS ONLY
*"A FEW ACRES
OF SNOW"*

PASSENGER PIGEONS
WERE ONCE SO PLENTIFUL
THAT HUGE FLOCKS WOULD HIDE
THE SUN FOR AN HOUR AT A TIME·
*THEY ARE NOW EXTINCT
BECAUSE THEY WERE RUTH-
LESSLY SLAUGHTERED FOR FOOD.*
THE LAST KNOWN PASSENGER
PIGEON DIED IN 1914

THE WORLD'S BIGGEST CHEESE

FULL SCALE PRODUCTION of DAIRY PRODUCTS — *CHEESE and BUTTER* — BEGAN in THE 1860's. By 1880 AN AMUSING DEVELOPMENT WAS THE COMPETITION in MAKING **LARGE CHEESES**.

THE GRAND CHAMPION was CALLED "THE **CANADIAN MITE**". MADE AT *Perth, Ont.*, IT WEIGHED 9.9 TONNES & WITH A CIRCUMFERENCE of 8.4 METRES IT STOOD 1.8 METRES IN HEIGHT

PAPERWORK THIS FESTIVE SEASON CANADIANS WILL USE OVER **96 000 Km** OF WRAPPING PAPER

Andrew BONAR LAW

BORN AT REXTON (KINGSTON), N.B. WAS THE *FIRST* AND ONLY *CANADIAN* TO BECOME *PRIME MINISTER* OF *GREAT BRITAIN.*

HE IS BURIED AMONG RENOWNED FIGURES OF BRITISH HISTORY IN WESTMINSTER ABBEY

THE **STEAM IRON** IS NOT THE MODERN INVENTION MANY PEOPLE THINK IT TO BE. *FROM 1860* ON THIS KIND OF "BEAUTY" WAS IN USE IN CANADA. IT WAS *CHARCOAL-FIRED* AND WORKED ON THE SAME PRINCIPLE AS ITS PRESENT DAY *ELECTRIC DESCENDANT*

JOHNSTON

ANGUS MACASKILL

THE CAPE BRETON GIANT

STOOD ALMOST 2.4 METRES TALL AND WEIGHED 225 Kg.

HE SMOKED A MALLET-SIZED PIPE THAT HELD A SIXTH OF A POUND OF TOBACCO AND DRANK RUM FROM A WOODEN BOWL THAT HELD THE EQUIVALENT OF THREE FULL GLASSES

THE DEATH PENALTY WAS IMPOSED FOR 11 CRIMES IN CANADA IN 1859 - ARSON BEING ONE OF THE CRIMES IN QUESTION

ALERT WEATHER STATION WAS ESTABLISHED IN **1950**.
AT THE TOP OF ELLESMERE ISLAND IT IS ONLY **800 Km** FROM THE NORTH POLE. HERE METEOROLOGISTS MAKE OBSERVATIONS IN THE UPPER AIR SEVERAL TIMES A DAY BY SENDING UP HYDROGEN BALLOONS THAT CARRY RADIO TRANSMITTERS THAT SIGNAL CONDITIONS OF WIND AND TEMPERATURE. *IT IS THE FURTHEST NORTH PERMANENT HUMAN HABITATION IN THE WORLD!*

C·B·C· ANNOUNCER
EARL CAMERON,

ONCE, WHILE READING THE NATIONAL RADIO NEWS, FOUND HIMSELF IN DARKNESS BECAUSE A BLOWN FUSE HAD DOUSED THE LIGHTS.

UNRUFFLED AS ALWAYS, CAMERON SIMPLY PULLED OUT HIS CIGARETTE LIGHTER, FLICKED IT ON AND CONTINUED TO READ

ANCIENT SEEDS OF THE <u>Arctic Lupin</u>

FOUND IN FROZEN SILT AT Miller Creek IN THE Yukon Territory, IN JULY, 1954, WERE ESTABLISHED TO BE OVER **10,000** YEARS OLD

EMMY – THE SHIPS CAT of THE C.P.R. LINER THE **Empress of Ireland**, HAD MADE MANY TRIPS ON THE EMPRESS UNTIL May 28, 1914 WHEN SHE LEFT THE SHIP AS IT PREPARED TO CAST OFF FROM Quebec City BOUND FOR ENGLAND. NOTHING WOULD INDUCE HER TO GO ABOARD AGAIN, EVEN THE FACT SHE WAS LEAVING A LITTER OF KITTENS. DURING THAT NIGHT, THE Empress WAS RAMMED BY ANOTHER SHIP IN DENSE FOG ON THE ST. LAWRENCE NEAR Rimouski – AND SHE SANK WITH A LOSS OF OVER A THOUSAND LIVES

©1970

THE SEWING MACHINE

WAS THE **FIRST** LABOR-SAVING DEVICE TO COME INTO THE HOME.

A POPULAR BRAND (SINGER) CAME TO CANADA IN 1867 AND WITH IT CAME THE **FIRST INSTALLMENT BUYING.**

ITS INVENTOR STARTLED THE WORLD BY SELLING HIS MACHINES FOR $5 DOWN & $3 A MONTH — WITH VERY FEW LOSSES

CIRCA 1908

A **PLAQUE** ERECTED AT ST. ANTHONY, NFLD. BY THE GREAT HUMANITARIAN SIR WILFRED GRENFELL, AFTER A HARROWING EXPERIENCE ON A DRIFTING ICE PAN.

GRENFELL HAD TO KILL THE DOGS TO USE THEIR BLOODY FUR FOR WARMTH UNTIL HE WAS RESCUED

TO THE MEMORY OF THREE NOBLE DOGS.
• MOODY •
• WATCH •
• SPY •
WHOSE LIVES WERE GIVEN FOR MINE ON THE ICE.
April 21st 1908.
WILFRED GRENFELL.
ST. ANTHONY

©1973

THE HON. GEORGE BROWN,

THE FOUNDER OF THE GLOBE (NOW GLOBE AND MAIL) NEWSPAPER WAS THE POLITICAL ARCH-ENEMY OF OUR FIRST PRIME MINISTER SIR JOHN A. MACDONALD, WHO SOMETIMES OVER-INDULGED HIS HABIT OF DRINKING.

WHENEVER MACDONALD HAD A BOUT WITH THE BOTTLE BROWN PRINTED A "SICK" NOTICE IN THE GLOBE

IN THE EARLY DAYS OF MOTORING ROADS WERE BAD, BUT THEY BECAME DEPLORABLE IN SPRINGTIME. AT ONE TIME ALL MOTOR TRAVEL WAS BANNED FOR 40 DAYS & 40 NIGHTS EVERY SPRING IN NOVA SCOTIA — TILL THE FROST CAME OUT OF THE GROUND

NO PLACE FOR WEAKLINGS

THOUSANDS OF GOLD SEEKERS SOUGHT TO REACH THE KLONDIKE DURING THE YUKON GOLD RUSH. TO CLIMB THE TREACHEROUS MOUNTAIN PASSES WAS DIFFICULT ENOUGH, *BUT TO HELP ENSURE THEIR SURVIVAL, THE MOUNTED POLICE WOULDN'T ALLOW THEM TO CROSS THE BORDER UNLESS EACH MAN TRANSPORTED A FULL TON OF SUPPLIES*

TURTLES WERE HONORED AS SYMBOLS OF BRAVERY BY MANY INDIAN TRIBES BECAUSE THEY DO NOT OFTEN TURN AWAY FROM DANGER

PERILOUS PAIRS KILLER WHALES SOMETIMES WORK AS A TEAM AND TWO OF THEM WILL GANG UP ON A *NARWHAL* AND CRUSH IT BETWEEN THEM

THE WORLD'S **HIGHEST TIDES** ARE FOUND ALONG THE BAY OF FUNDY BETWEEN NOVA SCOTIA AND NEW BRUNSWICK

VANCOUVER - PREVIOUSLY CALLED Gastown, WAS ALMOST ENTIRELY LEVELLED BY FIRE THE YEAR IT WAS INCORPORATED - 1886

A **DEAD SHARK** SINKS SO SLOWLY THAT ITS BODY IS LITERALLY DISSOLVED BY THE SALT IN THE WATER BEFORE IT REACHES THE FLOOR OF THE OCEAN. THE ONLY PART OF THE SHARK THAT IS IMPERMEABLE TO THE ACTION OF THE SALT IS ITS TEETH

©1970

HUCKLEBERRY FINN

THE HERO OF *MARK TWAIN'S* FAMOUS NOVEL *"THE ADVENTURES OF HUCKLEBERRY FINN"* IS ONE OF THE MOST BELOVED CHARACTERS IN AMERICAN FOLKLORE...

4-8

... U.S. PUBLISHERS AND REVIEWERS REJECTED IT OUT-RIGHT, AND IT WAS ONLY *AFTER* IT HAD BEEN *PUBLISHED* IN CANADA THAT IT WAS FINALLY ACCEPTED IN THE U.S.A.

ANOTHER HUMAN CAUSED TRAGEDY IN OUR FORESTS

SOMETHING IS HAPPENING IN CANADA TODAY THAT IS RELATIVELY NEW. FREQUENTLY IT HAS SAD CONSEQUENCES

PEOPLE ON CAMPING TRIPS OR JUST PLAIN PICNICING, COOK FOODS IN FOIL WRAPPERS, THEN LEAVE THE FOIL LYING ABOUT OR BURY IT TOO SHALLOWLY.

WILD ANIMALS FINDING FOOD RESIDUE IN THIS MANNER EAT FOIL AND ALL. NATURALLY, THE FOIL REMAINS IN THEIR STOMACHS AND CAUSES SLOW AGONIZING DEATHS

A COPY OF DICKEN'S *PICKWICK PAPERS* ...

...WAS FOUND IN A GARBAGE DUMP, AND RETURNED TO THE KINGSTON, ONT. PUBLIC LIBRARY...

...42 YEARS *OVERDUE.*

THE UNPAID FINE IS CALCULATED AT $604.00

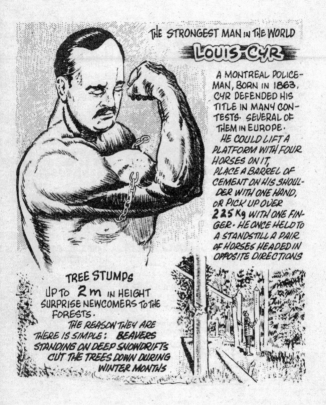

THE STRONGEST MAN IN THE WORLD
LOUIS CYR

A MONTREAL POLICE-
MAN, BORN IN 1863,
CYR DEFENDED HIS
TITLE IN MANY CON-
TESTS. SEVERAL OF
THEM IN EUROPE.
HE COULD LIFT A
PLATFORM WITH FOUR
HORSES ON IT,
PLACE A BARREL OF
CEMENT ON HIS SHOUL-
DER WITH ONE HAND,
OR PICK UP OVER
225 Kg WITH ONE FIN-
GER. HE ONCE HELD TO
A STANDSTILL A PAIR
OF HORSES HEADED IN
OPPOSITE DIRECTIONS

TREE STUMPS
UP TO 2 m IN HEIGHT
SURPRISE NEWCOMERS TO THE
FORESTS.
THE REASON THEY ARE
THERE IS SIMPLE: BEAVERS
STANDING ON DEEP SNOWDRIFTS
CUT THE TREES DOWN DURING
WINTER MONTHS

HOW PREHISTORIC WEALTH WAS FOUND

IN PRE-CONFEDERATION DAYS, PROSPECTORS CROSSING NORTHERN ONTARIO WERE PUZZLED BY THE FACT THAT THEIR COMPASSES SPUN CRAZILY IN THE AREA OF PRESENT DAY SUDBURY.

THE MYSTERY WAS SOLVED IN THE '80's WHEN CONSTRUCTION GANGS WERE DYNAMITING THEIR WAY THROUGH PRE-CAMBRIAN ROCK TO LAY A ROAD BED FOR THE C.P.R. THEY FOUND NICKEL DEPOSITS SO VAST IN SCOPE THAT IT STAGGERED THE IMAGINATION OF THE WORLD

THE COAT OF ARMS OF THE HUDSON'S BAY COMPANY IS EMBLAZONED WITH 2 ELKS & 4 BEAVERS, WHICH IS WHAT THE RENT CONSISTS OF —IF THE QUEEN COMES TO COLLECT IT

SANDY McINTYRE

DURING THE EARLY DAYS OF NORTHERN ONTARIO'S GOLD RUSH (1909), McINTYRE FOUND WHAT IS NOW THE FAMOUS MINE BEARING HIS NAME. HE SOLD OUT FOR $25 IN ORDER TO BUY SOME LIQUOR. 4 YEARS LATER ... HE STILL PASSED HIS TIME CRYING IN BEVERAGE ROOMS WHILE THE MINE HE DISCOVERED PRODUCED GOLD WORTH **230 MILLION DOLLARS**

TWO CARS THAT COLLIDED ON AN **ICY** ROAD AT **Ajax,** Ont. WERE OWNED BY DRIVERS NAMED **BLIZZARD** AND **SNOW**

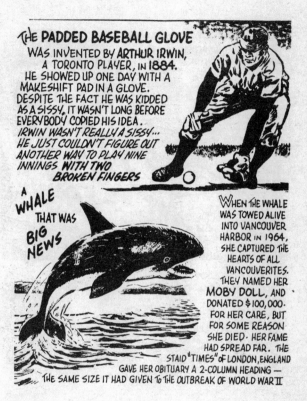

THE PADDED BASEBALL GLOVE

WAS INVENTED BY ARTHUR IRWIN, A TORONTO PLAYER, IN 1884. HE SHOWED UP ONE DAY WITH A MAKESHIFT PAD IN A GLOVE. DESPITE THE FACT HE WAS KIDDED AS A SISSY, IT WASN'T LONG BEFORE EVERYBODY COPIED HIS IDEA. IRWIN WASN'T REALLY A SISSY... HE JUST COULDN'T FIGURE OUT ANOTHER WAY TO PLAY NINE INNINGS *WITH TWO BROKEN FINGERS*

A WHALE THAT WAS BIG NEWS

WHEN THE WHALE WAS TOWED ALIVE INTO VANCOUVER HARBOR IN 1964, SHE CAPTURED THE HEARTS OF ALL VANCOUVERITES. THEY NAMED HER MOBY DOLL, AND DONATED $100,000. FOR HER CARE, BUT FOR SOME REASON SHE DIED. HER FAME HAD SPREAD FAR. THE STAID "TIMES" OF LONDON, ENGLAND GAVE HER OBITUARY A 2-COLUMN HEADING — THE SAME SIZE IT HAD GIVEN TO THE OUTBREAK OF WORLD WAR II

THE YUKON ICE WORM COCKTAIL

DURING THE YUKON GOLD RUSH, ANY GREENHORN VISITING THE MALMUTE SALOON, WHO BRAGGED ABOUT HIS ACCOMPLISHMENTS AS A SOURDOUGH WAS ASKING TO BE TAKEN DOWN A PEG OR TWO.

THIS WAS DONE BY HAVING HIM DRINK A SPECIALLY PREPARED COCKTAIL; THE CHIEF INGREDIENT OF WHICH WAS AN "ICE WORM".

NO GREENHORN WAS EVER TOLD THE 'WORM' WAS A FOOD-COLORED INCH OF SPAGHETTI WITH INK DOT EYES

A **BEE** IN GATHERING **ONE POUND** OF **HONEY** FLIES A DISTANCE THAT IS EQUIVALENT TO TWICE *AROUND THE WORLD AT THE EQUATOR* — *80 000 Km*

AN EARLY SNOWMOBILE IN MANITOBA

A CONVERTED MODEL "T" RAN FOR A TRANSPORTATION COMPANY BETWEEN THE PAS AND FLIN FLON — 1928

A **GLASS HOUSE** SHAPED LIKE A CASTLE IS THE HOME OF **GEORGE PLUMB**, NEAR *COWICHAN, BRITISH COLUMBIA.* THE OUTSIDE WALLS CONSIST OF OVER **200,000** EMPTY BOTTLES ENCASED IN CONCRETE

RURAL TELEPHONE SYSTEMS

ON THE PRAIRIES WERE IN OPERATION YEARS BEFORE RADIO AND WERE USED AS A FORM OF PASTIME.

BEING PARTY LINES IT WAS TAKEN FOR GRANTED THAT EVERYONE ON THE LINE LISTENED IN.

THEY WERE INVALUABLE AS INSTRUMENTS OF INSTANT COMMUNICATION. ONE LONG EXTENDED RING WAS THE SIGNAL FOR EVERYONE TO ANSWER. BY THIS METHOD NEWS OF PUBLIC MEETINGS, DANCES, AUCTION SALES, DEATHS, FIRES, ETC. WAS PASSED ALONG

A BOTTLE

THROWN INTO THE ATLANTIC FROM A SHIP OUTBOUND FROM HALIFAX IN 1906 WAS PICKED UP 2½ YEARS LATER IN THE BAY OF GUICHEN, SOUTH AUSTRALIA, HAVING TRAVELED 21 000 KM AND CROSSING BOTH THE ATLANTIC AND INDIAN OCEANS

THE BEAR THAT WAS EATEN WITH ITS OWN TEETH

NIMROD ROBERTSON, WHO HAD LOST ALL HIS TEETH TO SCURVY ARRIVED OVER THE DANGEROUS CHILKOOT PASS TO PROSPECT DURING THE YUKON GOLD RUSH. WITH HIM HE HAD SPECIALLY PREPARED FOOD AND ONE DAY A BEAR BROKE INTO HIS CACHE AND ATE IT ALL UP. NOT WANTING TO RECROSS THE CHILKOOT PASS FOR MORE FOOD, ROBERTSON SET TRAPS AND CAUGHT "ONE OF THE BIGGEST BLACK BEARS EVER SEEN IN THE YUKON"— THEN HE SET TO WORK. AFTER FIRING UP A FORGE HE EXTRACTED THE BEAR'S TEETH. THEN HE MELTED HIS TIN CUP, AND USING CLAY AND SPRUCE RESIN FOR MOLDS HE POURED IN THE MOLTEN METAL AND SET THE BEAR'S TEETH IN TO FASHION A SET OF FALSE TEETH. *DURING THE REMAINDER OF THE WINTER HE ATE THE BEAR WITH ITS OWN TEETH*

A MERCURIAL MONEY-MARKET

DURING THE EARLY DAYS OF ALBERTA'S OIL INDUSTRY, EVERY NOOK AND CRANNY IN DOWNTOWN CALGARY WAS ADAPTED FOR OFFICE SPACE FOR THE SALE OF NEW STOCK ISSUES. AT THE END OF EACH BOOMING BUSINESS DAY MONEY HAD TO BE CARTED TO THE BANKS IN BIG CARDBOARD BOXES AND GARBAGE CANS

THE HORRIBLE HUMP
IN QUEBEC CITY

IN HER 360 YEAR HISTORY, Quebec City HAS SUFFERED MUCH FROM FIRES AND LANDSLIDES.

ON SEVERAL OCCASIONS SERIOUS LANDSLIDES OCCURRED AT Quebec WITH HEAVY LOSS of LIFE.

IN 1889, WITH A THUNDERING ROAR, A GREAT MASS of THE 90 m ROCK CLIFF TOWERING OVER LOWER TOWN CRASHED DOWN ON HOUSES NESTLING BELOW, CRUSHING THEM LIKE EGGSHELLS.

TODAY A PERCEPTIBLE HUMP ON Champlain Street IS EVIDENCE OF THE VOLUME OF ROCK THAT FELL OVER 80 YEARS AGO. IT WAS FOUND EASIER TO RECONSTRUCT THE ROAD OVER A LARGE PART OF THE MASS THAN TO REMOVE IT

THE PIONEER ACADIAN CHRISTMAS FEAST WAS "GARTEAU"

– A HUGE, RICH, FLAKY CRUSTED PIE CONTAINING RABBITS, BIRDS AND PORK

AN OLD WORM-EATEN FRANCISCO GOYA SKETCHBOOK

ONCE AUCTIONED IN VICTORIA FOR $20.00

IT WAS LATER VALUED AT $465,000.00

OOLIKAN FISH WERE USED BY NATIVE PEOPLE and EARLY SETTLERS of BRITISH COLUMBIA — AS CANDLES

THE MAN WHO TOOK A TRIP THROUGH THE BOWELS OF AN AVALANCHE

IN Mar.1910, William Lachance, FIREMAN OF A SNOW-CLEARING WORK TRAIN in *ROGER'S PASS, B.C.** HAD NO TIME TO BE ASTONISHED WHEN SNOW EXPLODED FROM THE FIRE-BOX INSTEAD of SEARING HEAT. THE NEXT INSTANT HE WAS ON HIS WAY ON AN INCREDIBLY FANTASTIC JOURNEY THROUGH THE CENTER OF A GIGANTIC AVALANCHE. CHURNED AND WHIRLED IN A BOILING MOTION FOR WHAT SEEMED AN ETERNITY, HE WAS SUDDENLY FLUNG CLEAR AS IF BY AN EXPLOSION, TO LAND ON TOP OF THE SNOW WHERE ALL HAD BECOME DEATHLY SILENT. MIRACULOUSLY HE SURVIVED THE AWFUL SLIDE — YET *58 MEMBERS OF THE TRAIN CREW & WORK GANG HAD PERISHED*

*ONE OF THE WORLD'S MOST AVALANCHE-PRONE AREAS

ANNUAL RAINFALL AT Ocean Falls, B.C. AVERAGES 375 cm

©1971 - JOHNSTON

SRAID NAH-EAGLAISE
CHURCH STREET.

BILINGUALISM

IN PUGWASH, NOVA SCOTIA MEANS *GAELIC AND ENGLISH*. STREET NAME SIGNS USE BOTH LANGUAGES

AT YELLOWKNIFE N.W.T.

FROM MID-JUNE TO MID-JULY *SUNSET* AND *SUNRISE* BLEND SO THAT IT IS POSSIBLE TO READ A PAPER OUT OF DOORS **AT MIDNIGHT**

GHOSTS ABOUND IN THE MARITIMES. ONE SEEN BY LITERALLY HUNDREDS OF PEOPLE AT SYDNEY, N.S. WAS THAT OF A YOUNG SOLDIER WHO HAD DIED. HIS BODY WAS OBTAINED BY A DOCTOR FOR DISSECTION PURPOSES. BUT FRIENDS OF THE DEAD SOLDIER MADE SUCH A STRONG OBJECTION TO THIS, THAT THE DOCTOR BURIED THE BODY IN HIS GARDEN. THERE, FOR MANY YEARS AFTERWARD THE SOLDIERS GHOST IS SAID TO HAVE PACED SENTRY DUTY— WITH BOTH ARMS SEVERED.

JOHNSTON

THE DAY REGINA *BLEW DOWN*

ON JUNE 30, 1912 A WHIRLING, TWISTING, SHRIEKING TORNADO HIT THE SOUTH SIDE OF REGINA LIKE A BLAST OF AN ATOMIC BOMB. IN SECONDS IT CUT A SIX-BLOCK WIDE PATH OF DEATH AND DESTRUCTION THROUGH THE CITY. LIKE A GIANT SLASHING LAWNMOWER IT SHEARED OFF BUILDINGS, CRUMPLED THEM, AND SPEWED OUT RUBBLE IN ITS WAKE. ONE MOMENT REGINA HAD BEEN A STURDY, COMPACT CITY: THE NEXT, MUCH OF IT WAS A SHAMBLES

DOG POWER

VARIOUS FOWL AND TYPES OF MEAT WERE ROASTED BEFORE THE FIRE OF EARLY QUEBEC KITCHEN FIREPLACES, BY PUTTING THEM ON THE SPIT WHICH WAS REVOLVED BY A SMALL DOG IN A CYLINDRICAL CAGE CONNECTED WITH THE SPIT

HORRID HUNDRED SECONDS

Disaster struck FRANK, ALBERTA on April 29, 1903, when a gigantic wedge of limestone 390m high, 1200m wide and 150m thick, crashed down from Turtle Mountain and destroyed the town. 63 MILLION TONNES OF ROCK swept over 3.2 Km of valley, taking 66 lives (the official count—there were many more) burying homes, mine plant, railway sidings and 1280 hectares of fertile land to a depth of 30m—all in 100 seconds

BLUEBERRIES
GROW AS BIG AS MARBLES
IN THE SAGUENAY AREA OF QUEBEC

The Hermit of Niagara

Francis Abbot appeared at Niagara Falls in 1829. He was fascinated by the "sea-green waters and unearthly spray".

Building a cabin on *Goat Island* on the brink of the gorge he retired to a life of seclusion, but often was seen with his hair streaming in the wind getting as close as possible to the wild torrents.

Then just 2 years after his arrival, Abbot entered the Niagara River as though driven by some inner compulsion and **11 days later the whirlpool gave up his drowned body**

GRUNT is a steamed pudding

—made with blueberries or other small fruits in the Maritimes. So named because of the sound it makes while boiling

CANADA'S FIRST MILITANT
FOR WOMEN'S LIBERATION

NELLIE MOONEY McCLUNG
of WINNIPEG

IN JANUARY 1914, LED A
VOCIFEROUS DELEGATION OF LADIES,
CAMPAIGNING FOR THE RIGHT TO VOTE,
INTO THE MANITOBA LEGISLATURE
FOR A CONFRONTATION WITH THE
PREMIER SIR RODMOND ROBLIN.
POLITELY REBUFFED BY THE
PREMIER, NELLIE McCLUNG AND
HER FOLLOWERS SHOWED THEY
MEANT BUSINESS BY PLYING THE
PROVINCE IN BUCKBOARDS AND
LUMBER WAGONS, GATHERING A
PETITION OF 44,000 SIGNATURES
— ENOUGH TO WIN THEM THE VOTE IN
1916. ALBERTA & SASKATCHEWAN
ALSO YIELDED THAT YEAR, AND MOST
PROVINCES SOON AFTER, THOUGH
QUEBEC WAITED UNTIL 1940

THE BROWN BAT

THRIVES ON FLYING INSECTS,
AND IS ABLE TO CATCH
1000 PER HOUR USING
ITS ULTRASONIC ECHO
LOCATION SOUNDS

CAPT. **ROALD AMUNDSEN,**
A NORWEGIAN,
IN 1906 COMPLETED
THE FIRST TRAVERSE
OF THE LONG SOUGHT
NORTHWEST PASSAGE
THROUGH THE POLAR SEAS,
IN HIS LITTLE SHIP
THE GJOA

AN EARLY
DO-IT-YOURSELF
PROJECT

AS EARLY AS 1902 HOME CRAFTS-
MEN WERE OFFERED A $500. KIT
(CRATES OF CHASSIS, BODY PARTS
AND ENGINE) WITH WHICH TO
BUILD A CAR CALLED A *DYKE*

THE GRAVEYARD OF THE ATLANTIC — SABLE ISLAND

OFF THE S:EAST COAST of NOVA SCOTIA IS GIVEN THAT DESCRIPTIVE TITLE BY MARINERS.

TODAY IT IS THE HOME OF WILD PONIES, BUT SINCE IT WAS FIRST CHARTED ABOUT 450 YEARS AGO IT HAS SNARED and DESTROYED OVER 500 SHIPS WITH A LOSS OF 10,000 LIVES. AUTHENTIC SOURCES SAY THAT $2,000,000. IN GOLD LIES IN SHIPS STRONGBOXES BENEATH THE BOILING SURFACE

THOMAS RICKETTS

— A PRIVATE IN THE ROYAL NEWFOUNDLAND REGIMENT DURING WORLD WAR I
— BECAME, AT AGE 17, THE YOUNGEST SOLDIER EVER TO WIN THE VICTORIA CROSS

THE FROZEN DUTCHMAN

Far in the Arctic on the shores of Frobisher Bay, a geodetic survey party in 1902 uncovered a tomb. It contained a dead man with papers identifying him as:

DERRICK VAN LAAN of HOLLAND, A WHALER, WHO DIED JULY 11, 1740. HE HAD REMAINED IN A PERFECTLY PRESERVED STATE FOR 162 YEARS. THE TOMB WAS RESEALED and PRESUMABLY DERRICK VAN LAAN REMAINS REFRIGERATED AFTER 234 YEARS

MACABRE MEMENTOES

When Dr. William King of Brighton, Ontario was hanged in 1859 for the murder of his wife, the relatives of the murdered woman cut up the hangman's rope and kept the pieces as souvenirs

MRS. **NANCY HODGES**

— WAS NAMED *SPEAKER* OF BRITISH COLUMBIA'S LEGISLATIVE ASSEMBLY IN 1949, AND THEREBY BECAME *THE FIRST WOMAN EVER TO HOLD THE SPEAKER'S CHAIR IN ANY CANADIAN PARLIAMENT*

SACRED TO THE MEMORY of CORPORAL JOSEPH HIBBERT COY K. 4TH REGIMENT NEW HAMPSHIRE INFANTRY KILLED IN ACTION MAY 16, 1864 AT THE BATTLE OF DREWRYS BLUFF, VIRGINIA

JOHNSTON

VETERANS of FOREIGN WARS

SOME OLDER GRAVESTONES IN CEMETERIES IN THE EASTERN TOWNSHIPS OF QUEBEC ARE STILL DECORATED WITH THE STARS & STRIPES OF THE U·S·A· THESE ARE THE GRAVES OF CANADIANS WHO FOUGHT FOR THE NORTHERN SIDE IN THE AMERICAN CIVIL WAR (1861-1865) · BEST ESTIMATES ARE THAT **40,000 CANADIANS** FOUGHT IN THE UNION ARMY

WHERE LIFE HANGS BY *A THREAD*

THE PROMETHEA MOTH PUPA

SPENDS THE WINTER IN A SILK SEWED LEAF — ATTACHED TO A THICKET BY A STRONG THREAD OF SILK

THE PHENOMENAL
SPOTTED LAKE

NEAR OSOYOOS, BRITISH COLUMBIA, IS ONE OF THE WORLD'S GREATEST CONCENTRATIONS OF MINERAL WATERS.

THE SPOTS ARE CAUSED BY ALMOST SOLID MINERALS FORMING SEPERATE CIRCULAR POOLS, SOME COLD, SOME HOT.

THE WATERS ARE SAID TO CONTAIN HEALING PROPERTIES

THE ROYAL CANADIAN NAVY...

...IN WHICH MANY PRAIRIE BOYS SERVED DURING WORLD WAR II, PLAYED A MAJOR ROLE IN THE BATTLE OF THE ATLANTIC.

BY THE WAR'S END IT HAD SAFELY ESCORTED OVER 25,000 MERCHANT SHIPS THROUGH U-BOAT INFESTED WATERS TO GT. BRITAIN

FROGS — HEAR WITH THEIR EYES. BEHIND EACH EYE IS A SMALL NERVE CONNECTED TO THE BRAIN

THE HUMAN POLAR BEAR **TROY FRIIS** OF QUEBEC CITY, EVEN WHEN THE TEMPERATURE IS WELL BELOW ZERO, CHOPS A HOLE IN THE ICE ON THE RIVER BESIDE HIS HOME, *THEN PLUNGES IN FOR AN EARLY MORNING DIP.*

AT AGE 60, HE HAS DONE IT EVERY WINTER OF HIS ADULT LIFE

KEITH McKENZIE CHIEF TRADER FOR THE HUDSON'S BAY COMPANY IN LABRADOR DURING THE 1890's COULD LIFT *A 22·5 kg WEIGHT WITH HIS LITTLE FINGER AND AT ARMS LENGTH WRITE HIS NAME ON A WALL*

THE MAN WHO WALKED 1280 Km TO MEET HIS BRIDE

EMIL VOGELSANG FRESH FROM GERMANY IN 1867 ESTABLISHED CANADA'S First BUTTON FACTORY —AT Berlin, NOW Kitchener, Ont.

WILBUR WOLFENDON —A DUTCH IMMIGRANT WALKED IN THE DEAD OF WINTER FROM Calgary TO Winnipeg TO MEET HIS PROSPECTIVE BRIDE, ARRIVING FROM HOLLAND—1908

THE ARCTIC TERN ALWAYS LAYS 3 EGGS THEN FLIES OVER ITS NEST CRYING "TRIEG" —NORWEGIAN FOR 3 EGGS

©1971 — JOHNSTON

"ITS AN ILL WIND that BLOWS"...

QUEBEC COMMUNISTS, BARRED FROM DISTRIBUTING PROPAGANDA PAMPHLETS — ONCE CAME UP WITH A NOVEL WAY to CIRCULATE LEAFLETS in QUEBEC CITY.

PARTY WORKERS SNEAKED BUNDLES OF HANDBILLS UP TO THE ROOFS OF DOWNTOWN BUILDINGS AND LET THE WIND SHOWER THEM OVER THE CITY

OYSTERS ARE BORN BY THE BILLIONS — YET ONLY ONE OYSTER in 145,000 REACHES MATURITY AT THE AGE OF TWO YEARS

A GOVERNOR WHO HAD SEEN A GHOST

ONE DAY IN 1785, LT·GEORGE WYNARD AND CAPT· JOHN SHERBROOKE (LATER GOVERNOR-IN-CHIEF OF CANADA –1816) WERE IN THE OFFICERS' MESS AT SYDNEY, N·S· THEY SAW A YOUNG CIVILIAN PASS THROUGH THE ROOM AND WYNARD EXCLAIMED IT WAS HIS BROTHER WHO WAS IN ENGLAND! BUT THEN, THE TWO PUZZLED OFFICERS WERE UNABLE TO FIND THE YOUNG MAN ANYWHERE ON THE PREMISES. LATER...

... SHERBROOKE RECEIVED A LETTER FROM ENGLAND ...

... ASKING HIM TO TELL WYNARD THAT HIS BROTHER HAD DIED — ON THE VERY DAY, AT THE VERY HOUR, HE HAD "APPEARED" IN SYDNEY

MYSTERIOUS ANCIENT COINS...

... WERE FOUND BY MINERS EXCAVATING A TUNNEL IN THE CASSIAR DISTRICT OF BRITISH COLUMBIA IN 1882.

TAKEN TO VICTORIA, THE MONEY WAS IDENTIFIED AS CURRENCY OF CHINA DATING FROM 2,000 B.C.

A FAST EXIT

SIR JOHN A. MacDONALD, OUR FIRST PRIME MINISTER

—FREQUENTLY AVOIDED PERSISTENT PATRONAGE-SEEKERS BY SLIPPING OUT OF HIS OFFICE BY A BACK DOOR AND DOWN A PRIVATE SPIRAL STAIRWAY TO THE STREET BELOW

Pieces of Congealed Mist FROM NIAGARA FALLS, SOLD AS SOUVENIRS FROM THE EARLIEST DAYS OF TOURISM AT THE FAMOUS SITE, WERE LITTLE WHITE STONES IMPORTED FROM ENGLAND

THE WEEKLY NEWSPAPERS HAVE *MORE* CANADIAN-CONTENT THAN ANY OTHER DIVISION OF THE MASS MEDIA

PRINCE ALBERT — THE FIRST WHITE SETTLEMENT IN SASKATCHEWAN, HAS ANOTHER IMPORTANT DISTINCTION. THREE OF ITS MEMBERS OF PARLIAMENT HAVE BEEN PRIME-MINISTERS (*LAURIER, KING* AND *DIEFENBAKER*) WHILE SITTING FOR THE CONSTITUENCY

THE DEATH OF THE GREAT HOUDINI

ONE OF THE WORLD'S GREATEST MAGICIANS AND A SUPERB SHOWMAN, HOUDINI ISSUED PUBLIC CHALLENGES. HE MADE FANTASTIC WAGERS AND PERFORMED DEATH-DEFYING FEATS, AND ONE OF HIS GREATEST BOASTS WAS THAT HE COULD TAKE A BLOW TO HIS STOMACH FROM ANY MAN. *IN 1926, IN MONTREAL, A McGILL STUDENT PUT THIS CLAIM TO THE TEST.*

THOUGH HE APPEARED TO RECOVER FROM THE STUDENT'S PUNCH, HOUDINI DIED WITHIN HOURS

BABY **DOLPHINS** — BEGIN TO LEAP ALONGSIDE THEIR MOTHERS *AS SOON AS THEY ARE BORN*

THE **BALD EAGLE**
IS THE NATIONAL SYMBOL OF THE U·S·A· — *YET MORE OF THEM EXIST IN BRITISH COLUMBIA THAN ALL OF THE STATES*

The Great AUK

A LARGE FLIGHTLESS BIRD THAT INHABITED THE COASTS OF THE NORTH ATLANTIC *PASSED OUT OF EXISTENCE ON JUNE 4, 1844.* ITS END WAS TRAGICALLY TYPICAL —A PAIR WAS DISCOVERED WITH AN EGG AND DESTROYED, AND *THIS WAS THE LAST PAIR*

THE STATUE THAT WENT ON A VACATION

ONE DAY IN *1838* A STATUE OF *JAMES WOLFE* DISAPPEARED FROM Quebec City, AND IT CREATED QUITE A MYSTERY. THEN, AFTER A LONG PERIOD OF TIME, THE MYSTERY WAS SOLVED. *A CRATE ARRIVED IN THE CITY ADDRESSED TO THE MAYOR. INSIDE WAS THE STATUE.* IT TURNED OUT THAT SOME BRITISH SAILORS THOUGHT THE "GENERAL" NEEDED A VACATION IN WARMER CLIMES AND HAD SPIRITED "HIM" AWAY — FOR A TOUR OF THE FAR EAST

Vanished Forest Monarchs

It is difficult today for visitors to the city of Vancouver, B.C. to visualize the thousands of giant trees that towered to the skies, less than a hundred years ago, where downtown Vancouver now stands. From the dawn of time they had stood, many over 90m high, as thick as fields of grain.

Joey

A two-year old Budgie owned by Mrs. Joseph Peterson of Nanaimo, B.C.

Has a vocabulary of 280 words

SPHERICAL SLUMBER

CHARLES & ABIGAIL **BOWERS** WERE THE FIRST SETTLERS OF OHIO, SHELBURNE COUNTY, NOVA SCOTIA.

ABIGAIL WAS KNOWN AS A RESOURCEFUL WOMAN WHO HAD SEVENTEEN CHILDREN. SHE SOLVED THE PROBLEM OF BEDS FOR THEM BY PUTTING HER TEN BOYS IN A ROUND BED — *WITH ALL THE BED COVERS MADE CIRCULAR IN ORDER TO PREVENT UNEQUAL PORTIONS*

THE MOST ENGLISH CITY IN NORTH AMERICA IS **VICTORIA** B.C.

TO THE DELIGHT OF THEMSELVES AND TOURISTS THE NATIVES HANG FLOWER BASKETS ON THE DOWNTOWN LAMPPOSTS

A MYSTERIOUS LEVITATION - 1880

TWO MEN WORKING IN A FIELD IN EAST KENT, ONT., HEARD A PECULIAR, LOUD NOISE NEARBY. TURNING THEY SAW BOULDERS AND STONES FLYING UPWARDS FROM AN AREA NEAR THEM. AFTER THE STONES FELL BACK TO THE GROUND, THEY INVESTIGATED THE SPOT — ABOUT 1·5m² — BUT FOUND NO TRACE OF AN EXPLOSION OR OTHER DISTURBANCE WHICH COULD HAVE FLUNG THE STONES HIGH IN THE AIR.

PROFITEERING

IN 1899, SEVEN CAST IRON STOVES BOUGHT FOR $29.50 EACH IN VANCOUVER WERE SOLD AT McLEOD, N.W.T. for $250.00 EACH

JOHN BUCHAN
GOVERNOR-GENERAL 1935-1940

WAS A *SKILLED* NOVELIST and A MAN OF LETTERS.
HE TOOK A KEEN INTEREST IN LITERATURE, AND IT WAS HE WHO INITIATED *THE GOVERNOR-GENERAL'S LITERARY AWARDS* THAT ARE NOW MADE ANNUALLY

CANADA'S MINI DESERT

A SMALL AREA. ROUGHLY **24 Km** BY **48 Km**, LYING TO THE SOUTH OF PENTICTON, BRITISH COLUMBIA IS A GENUINE DESERT. ONLY FLORA & FAUNA THAT ARE TYPICAL OF DESERT ENVIRONMENT EXIST HERE, INCLUDING PRICKLY PEAR CACTUS AND RATTLESNAKES

ITS ANNUAL RAINFALL — LITTLE MORE THAN **19 cm** — IS ACTUALLY LESS THAN THAT OF THE SAHARA DESERT

LINUS, A CLYDESDALE HORSE IN FREDERICTON, N.B., HAD HAIR TO SPARE. MANE, 4·2 m LONG; FORETOP, 3 m LONG; TAIL, 3·7 m — 1920

100 YEARS AGO, CANADIAN NEWSPAPERS CARRIED STORIES ABOUT THE HIGH RENT RATES FOR HOUSES IN TORONTO, MAKING IT DIFFICULT FOR CLERKS AND MECHANICS TO OBTAIN DECENT HOUSING. *THE AVERAGE RATE AT THE TIME WAS $150. A YEAR*

SHOCK

...WAS PRESCRIBED AS A CURE FOR THE PARALYZED SPINE OF MRS. *Jean Fry Finigan*.

THE GREAT HALIFAX EXPLOSION IN 1917 WAS THE SHOCK THAT COMPLETELY CURED THE THEN 22 YEAR OLD GIRL

GOING TO GREAT LENGTHS

IN THE DAYS OF THE BIG SAILING SHIPS NOVA SCOTIA HAD A FLEET THAT COVERED EVERY OCEAN. BEGINNING AT Yarmouth IN 1763 TO THE END OF THE 19TH CENTURY THIS PROVINCE WAS A WORLD LEADER IN SHIP BUILDING AND SAILING.

THE ROPE RIGGINGS FOR SAIL CONTROL OF A TYPICAL WINDJAMMER OF THIS ERA TOTALLED ABOUT 29 Km IN LENGTH

THE ERA OF THE HOBOS

DURING THE 1930's THOUSANDS OF MEN TRAVELED ACROSS AND TO ALL PARTS OF CANADA ON THE TOPS OF FREIGHT TRAIN CARS SEEKING JOBS THAT JUST WEREN'T OBTAINABLE.

THE "GREAT DEPRESSION" BEGAN WITH THE CRASH OF THE NEW YORK STOCK MARKET IN 1929 AND CONTINUED UNTIL WORLD WAR II BROKE OUT 10 YEARS LATER. AT ITS HEIGHT IN 1933, MORE THAN 1,500,000 OUT OF CANADA'S TOTAL POPULATION OF 10,500,000 WERE ON WELFARE.

IT HAD BEEN 10 YEARS OF YOUTHFUL STAGNATION AND STARVATION WAGES

A MYSTERY ANCHOR

EARLY IN THE 19TH CENTURY A BRITISH SAILING SHIP NAMED "WAVE" SANK OFF THE COAST OF THE GASPÉ PENINSULA.

NEARLY A HUNDRED YEARS LATER ITS ANCHOR WAS FOUND IN HAMILTON BAY IN LAKE ONTARIO

WORLD BASKETBALL CHAMPIONS WITHOUT PEER

THE EDMONTON GRADS

LET'S FACE IT MEN! THE BEST GROUP IN THE ENTIRE HISTORY OF SPORTS IN CANADA WAS A TEAM OF GIRL BASKETBALL PLAYERS, CALLED THE EDMONTON GRADS. FROM 1915 TO 1940, UNDER THEIR COACH, PERCY PAGE, THEY UTTERLY DESTROYED ALL COMPETITION IN CANADA, THE USA AND EUROPE — WINNING 502 OF 522 GAMES, INCLUDING 27 OF THE 27 THEY PLAYED IN OLYMPIC TOURNAMENTS. IN 1940, WITH NO ONE LEFT TO DEFEAT, THEY DISBANDED

COLOR CHOICE?

PURCHASERS of EARLY FORD CARS WERE TOLD THEY COULD HAVE ANY COLOR THEY WANTED — SO LONG AS IT WAS **BLACK**

THE **TURKEY** IS KNOWN AS THE **AMERICAN BIRD** IN TURKEY

©1970

A RESCUE RECORD

IN A PERIOD OF 40 YEARS, **REG. GAUDAUR,** A BOATMAN ON OFTEN TREACHEROUS Lake Simcoe (56 Km N. of Toronto), SAVED MORE THAN **60** PERSONS FROM DROWNING

JACQUES CARTIER, LIKE MANY EUROPEANS OF HIS TIME, **DIED OF THE PLAGUE**

©1970- JOHNSTON

A SIGNIFICANT MILESTONE

WAS PASSED IN 1953 — FOR THE FIRST TIME *OIL PRODUCTION* ($198 MILLION) *EXCEEDED* THE VALUE OF *GOLD PRODUCTION* ($140 MILLION).

BLUE MOON

ON SEPT. 26, 1950, AN 200 000 KM² FOREST FIRE IN BRITISH COLUMBIA CAUSED SULPHUR PARTICLES TO FORM IN THE UPPER ATMOSPHERE.

BECAUSE OF THIS, THE MOON LOOKED *BLUE* TO VIEWERS IN GT. BRITAIN

WHITE HART